Help Me Into The Light
"GUIDE FOR THE AFTER LIFE"

AUTHOR
SENSITIVE/ EMPATHIC
BILLIE J. PEEL

Help Me Into The Light; "Guide For The Afterlife"
Copyright © 2010 by Billie Peel

Written in the United States Of America

Author's Bio

I was born in Chicago, Illinois as one of three daughters to an average American family. Since the early age of 5, I could see, sense spirits and their emotions and needs. I am, what is referred to as a Empathic /Sensitive. I also in my life, had very spontaneous premonitions of events that have taken place. The seclusion, ridicule and isolation that comes with having this unusual gift was painful. It wasn't until last 10 years I decided to become a paranormal investigator and let the world see me as I naturally was. My decision to write books pertaining to the supernatural came from those experiences as a child and my desire to express my knowledge into words for the world to read.

Billie Peel

Book Dedication:

To my husband , Jack Stuart Peel, who had inspired me to write this, without his support, faith, encouragement and love I would never have written this book. He believes that people need to know the truth and be prepared for the afterlife. So to him I say, "Thank you ".

Table of Contents

Chapter 1
"My Gift"

I am a sensitive/empathic/psychic. Six generations of my family had, or now have some sort of special talent relating to the gift of seeing, hearing, knowing or feeling, the paranormal world. My grandmother, father, I, my daughter and now my grandson all have this gift...

My grandmother was so very psychic she could tell you what you were thinking while the family was in the car, going to visit her. She knew what horse would win at the racetrack but because of her religious beliefs, self-righteousness and honesty, would not tell my grandfather what horse would win, so he could bet on it. She had the automatic writing, in which your hand moves involuntary and can write supposed messages from the beyond onto paper. She saw spirits from her early childhood and had very spontaneous premonitions of future events such as a ship sinking of which it did. She was suppose to sail on that ship as a child but pleaded with her mother to not take it to go to America, so they ended up going on an old barge/cargo ship instead. She knew and saw everything, as did her mother before her, my great grandmother.

Now my fathers' abilities were quite limited yet obvious. He could not go into a house where someone had died, as he would smell an overpowering aroma of roses. He also had memories of a past life as a soldier during the revolutionary war and strong memories of dying then and how it had happened. He remembered his last moments of life from his past life, which stayed with him until he passed away in this one.

My daughter senses and has seen spirits around her. Just like me they follow her where-

ever she relocates to. She is tormented by their attempts to get her attention, with bangs and/or movement, visual shadows or even vocal sounds, sometimes being that of a grunt or growl.

My grandson has seen two spirits, before the age of 8. One being of an angry elderly man and another of a woman in a yellow dress. He now has an intense fear of the dark because of that.

As for myself, I have been overwhelmed and tormented by spirits starting at the early age of five. I would see them on a weekly basis whether at night or in broad daylight. I feared sleeping so dearly that I would sit on the floor, next to my bed, leaning on it and hide under the blankets on the side. Hoping the spirits would not find me. I did not get much sleep as a child! The spirits followed me my whole life, everywhere I went so there is no escaping them.

Unfortunately, for me, my aura resembles the "Light" or the "Way" to the deceased, which seems to attract them in. They feel I can help them or save them. I have never actually heard them vocally, except for some very small occasions as a child, as it all seems visual and sensory to me. As an Empath, I feel their pain, joy or anger, their emotions as opposed to hearing them.

It is not just the dead I can read from, but the living also. I can sense if someone is good or not. Especially their intentions when it comes to confronting me. I also can sense if they have spirits around them and sometimes whom it is. I have given many readings to people who have a spirit following them to help remove it and bring closure. Most of the time it's just a deceased family member who wants to either give a message, apologize and/or needs help moving on. Most spirits are benign, very tame, just people like us, who just no longer have a body. They carry with them the same emotions as they had in life.

Also, as an empathic I feel the living and their pain or discomfort from being sick. I have been sick my entire life and never could understand why I had so many diseases and illness till just recently. I not only feel others pain but actually inherit their ailments! Alternatively, so I speculate. I did not really realize this until I went to visit my 85 year old mother. Her foot swelled considerably, so we brought her to the hospital and she was diagnosed with gout. Next day when I was at home, my foot swelled up! This has never happened before and was suspiciously similar to my mothers' foot swelling. When my mothers' foot stopped swelling so did mine...

If it is true I do pick up others ailments from being an empath, then it helps to explain my abnormally long history of unexplained illnesses and ailments. This is all speculation on my part and needs further investigating.

Now besides seeing spirits, sensing others pain both living and dead, I also have very spontaneous premonitions of future events usually but not confined to, bad events. Through out my life, I have foreseen events that would happen and they always unfolded just as I had predicted. I call these events very spontaneous for the reason I do NOT see all events that have befallen upon us. When I get a vision of an event to happen thou, it usually appears to me in the way of a movie playing before my eyes. Sometimes, I get them as a very persistent thought, I just cannot get rid of. When either of those events takes place, I know it's time to pay attention, that it is going to happen. Then it always does.

You should now be getting an idea of who I am, what I can do and how it was inherited in my family genes. Hopefully this will help you to understand the further you read into the book, what roles these gifts have given me in association to how I could possibly know so much about the afterlife, because of them.

Chapter 2
'Why this book is necessary"

Unless you are in my line of work and have the same psychic ability as I do, you perhaps could not understand the total extent of what is on the other side and what you may have to face in the here after…

Because of my sensitivity and being an empath I can feel what they, the deceased are going through. They are drawn to me as if I were a beacon, all seeking the same thing, help to move on. Though it may sound all so simple, as it is just a matter of going into the light after one dies, it in actuality is not. Death is just as complicated at times, as in life; you face the same tribulations and trials. You must find a home, you must behave, you must feel remorse if you have sinned .You make some of the same decisions in death as you do now in life. There are added concerns that you will face that are different in nature because of the fact you no longer will have a physical body to utilize. You will learn a new way of functioning, traveling and communication.

The pre-entry period before your dissension into the light will be more complex. You would be torn between the living world of which you just exited and the spiritual existence waiting for you on your plane in heaven. Therefore, you will not have the experience of how to function correctly until you go into the light. You may try intensely and very unsuccessfully to be alive again or should I say, behave physically alive again. If you are earthbound and have not moved on yet into the light you will find that no one can hear you that is living. Your hands will not open doors, as you no longer have human substance of flesh, bones fingers and muscles.

To interact with the physical world will be virtually

impossible. You feel and are still so very real, but just without your physical body. This may cause you to feel lost, lonely and uncomfortable, as you are resided between two worlds not yet crossed over into the light. You may walk or fall through walls, floors or float to whatever destinations you may want to. Your soul is light and free, without any weight.

At this point, you will diligently try to find a place you can live in, where you belong. You will feel a strong urge to go home and may confuse this urge with your past earthly home. We all have a place we call home on earth, but we also are designated a home on a heavenly plane in heaven. You must find that new home, after your earthly passing. Being bound to your earthly existence will weigh down your soul and not let you move on.

I have learned all this from the hundreds of EVPs or spirit voices, I have captured so easily from those who have been drawn to me and need my help to move on. They tell me of what they are going through and most are cries for help, as they do not know where to go or how to get there. They are only acknowledge by each other, other spirits that have also died. Once they find each other, they may travel together trying to find help or a way to move into the light. Only with each other, can they see or hear one another and it gives them a sense of security. Once again, they feel acknowledge in a physical sense, but not quite. It takes some of the loneliness away at that particular pre-entry moment.

I will not say you do not feel pain, until you descend into the light there may be some discomfort. You may feel cold or odd sensations, but mostly you should be pain free. You will be happy at some of the new experiences you will encounter, as flying freely can be a luxury. You can also walk, as a spirit, but you cannot be physically seen walking.

This stage, pre-entry to heaven, is exactly the reason

why this book is necessary. We all need to be prepared for this, but unfortunately until this book; there have been no instructions on what to do once you die. It serves as a learning tool and manual for your afterlife.

We need to remember, death is a part of life and as with all things in life; it helps to have a basic concept of what to do before you attempt to do it. You would not build a house or fix a sink, without first having read up on how to do so. If you did not research, you would end up with some nasty surprises and disheartening disappointments with the house you tried to build.

So, it is just as important to enter into your "Afterlife", with the knowledge of what to expect, how to improve and some of the unexpected surprises may be handled in a more educated and prepared manner. This will alleviate the fear factor and sense of being lost and disorientated. It will also guide you into an easier transition into the light with fewer problems.

For all the above-mentioned reasons, this is exactly why this book is necessary.

Chapter 3
"What holds the soul here after death"

Because I am a sensitive with empathic qualities, I draw deceased Souls to me. To them I resemble the "Light" or the "Way". These lost souls who seemly are trapped here on earth, have trouble moving on for various reasons.

I am fortunate enough to be able to connect with them using a technique of recording their voices, or audio analyzing, by using, a microphone hooked up to my computer and also the use of an appropriate, "Audio editing software". With this, I collect what is called "EVPS" or "Electronic Voice Phenomenon". In more basic, simpler terms, this means "Spirit voices". "Evps" are not hard for me to collect as the souls are unusually drawn to me and present for a session. I teach them how to speak loud into the microphone and other basics they need to know of how to get their voices across when they no longer have the use of a voice box. Its abit harder and very testing for them, as they have to learn a completely new way of speech or speaking.

I ask them questions pertaining to their physical death, life and the problems they now face moving on. I get some incredible answers or "EVPS" to my questions. With the information, they give me and with my empathic, sensitive trait, I am able to piece together what has held them here and therefore I can work on their problems, issues of containment to help them move on.

Most of my "EVPS" are a cry for help, as they do not know where to go. These can be common issues for one who has passed from their physical body, as there are no books on death itself, informing us what to do or where to go after death.

Now this does not happen to all newly deceased souls just the ones who are bound to something on earth of which may be of their own doing. The light is present to all good and yes, even not so good, when we first leave our body, but the confusion, adjustment to death can cause us to miss it or not be drawn to it. Once it's gone, its harder to find it again .Especially, if ones soul does not want to give up their earthly existence for one reason or another.

Its not that finding the light again is impossible, it's just that we have to let go of what holds us here in order to help us move on.

Being dead is not painful, I find that it is almost joyful at times, as I have many "EVPS" of them singing or having a good time conversing with each other. They hold their same personalities in death as they had in their physical life, of which I will talk of in another chapter within this book.

The real issues they have, the earthbound souls, are being unable to move on once they have missed the initial light. A decision basically has not been made or should have been made, on their part to let go. As long as they are bound to something, they cannot let go of, due mainly because of lack of education on how to let go, they become trapped. Physical life is heavy and bounding…Spiritual life is more light and free.

What makes our physical life so heavy is our unusual, or usual, attachment to a person(s), place, employment or thing, as in an object or objects. In addition, emotions can weigh us down, the one of guilt being the heaviest so saying your sorries before death, I highly recommend. These weights in physical life are carried by some into spiritual death, thus holding us here. Therefore, making us become earthbound.

Suicide will definitely leave the soul earthbound; it should never be an option to leave life. It is a sin. Ignorance of, not having a belief in, or a religion of ,a "Being greater than us" A god like entity, or any religion or likeness of the same, can cause one not to see the light after our passing...As greatness is the light. If you do not think greatness, you will not see the light. Some do not move on because they fear the light. Maybe they felt they were not all so good in life and may be punished. Truth being ,if once you die, if you have been incredibly bad in life , your soul will be grabbed right away and dragged down to where one so evil belongs. So if you have been dead for a while and nothing like that has happened...you are safe to go into the light.

The light is good and redeeming in nature. You will not be punished.

With an adult, who have died the reasons for being earthbound can be obvious. However, when a child who passes and does not go into the light, the reasons may be pediatric in nature. There is lack of religion, in some cases, due to the child's early passing, which may render the child unsure of a "God", or who to ask for help if they become lost. In addition, a child is taught commitment to their parents and not to venture anywhere without asking a parent first or getting permission.

Therefore, a child's spirit can therefore be trapped, as cruelly as that sounds, because of lack of parental permission to move on. So, if one has a child , who is incurably ill or terminal, it is best to tell them to call for "God" to show them the light if they get lost and too not be afraid to go into the light that they will see you someday within it. Give them permission to move on before hand.

I know it will be hard for you to do that but it is essential for their passing into the light. An angel may greet them and hold their hand into it (light); however, a fear of strangers because of the child cautionary teachings in life could cause them to pull away. Waiting for mommies or daddies permission and guidance after a child dies, is not a good thing.

What's necessary in life may not be important in death. Teach them to call to "God" and tell them to go into the light. That is the best gift you can give them for their passing. Honesty is important.

Therefore, to review what you should do or not do after death is…

1. Say your sorries before you're passing if possible.

2. At first passing, as disorientating as it may seem…look for a light or call "GOD" to show it to you. If you see, it let go of any earthly thoughts immediately and move into it.

3. Do not think or feel obliged to any person, place, job or things you had on earth. For that will weigh you down.

4. Do not fear the light as it will help you and stabilize your new spiritual existence on a heavenly plane.

5. Do not hold back from moving on as you think you may live again, which would be obviously impossible.

6. If for some reason, you do not see the light even after several calls to "GOD" for help…you must find out what it is you need to let go of to move on. Then either ask forgiveness for a sin to alleviate the guilt or give up your unusual attachment to something or someone on earth holding you down. Do not worry true love is free spirited and will not die it will go with you.

7. If it is a child passing, inform them to call to "God" to show them the light.

8. Also, tell them they got your permission to go into the light and ask God for it.

Chapter 4
"Paying for your sins in the Afterlife"

After you die, you may have to face your redeemable sins or mistakes head on. You will be your own trial and jury. Self-induced punishment will be your sentence for such crimes. Every act in life of selfishness, greed and violence towards another person, which you committed in your lifetime, will become a weight to your soul. Therefore, you have to deal with these weights before being able to move into the light.

After death you will feel guilt ridden. Every bad deed or evil act against another will face you head on. What I mean by this is, the acknowledgment of such acts will be enhanced, making you more conscious of what you did. Sometimes the simplest, smallest of insults to another living being may be brought forward in your subconscious as a obstacle to face and redeem. Name-calling, prejudice and cruel insults would be included in this. This could be the smallest of cruel acts that in life seemed quite trivial and forgettable at the time to you.

You enter therefore into a state of guilt, rendering you into a trial stage of seeking forgiveness. Since communication to the living once you have passed is impossible, a barrier will form. There will be no logical way for you to apologize to the victim of your cruelty. The weight will lay heavy on your soul rendering you earthbound until you can find a solution for redeeming yourself. Moving into the light in such a state, is virtually impossible. Unless you have a strong belief of a being greater and forgiving, you will not move on.

It's imperative you realize there is a greater being and the only way to relieve these weights is to confess all your sins, as minor as they may seem, and ask for forgiveness.

Steps to being forgiven are,

1. Acknowledgment of cruel acts.

2. Going through a guilt/ regret stage.

3. Reviewing to yourself why they were bad and how it affected others.

4. Confession and asking for forgiveness to a greater being such as "God". In some cases, it may take several pleas for forgiveness to "God", so you may need to call for him several times.

5. Ask for God to please show you and allow you to go into the light.

If you sins are beyond redeemable, you may go to a place not too pleasant, Hell, to pay restitution for them. This is usually the case if you committed a cold-blooded act of murder or torture, upon another human being, without any reasonable cause for such brutal acts. By reasonable cause, I mean in certain acts of self-defense. Being sentenced to a term in Hell will be carried out immediately after your mortal physical passing. The minute you pass from your life, the boughs of Hell will come up to claim your soul rendering you helpless. You may be grabbed by several evil entities and pulled below. This is a fact.

So, if you have died, knew you had sinned and have not instantly been grabbed to serve your just reward for such sins, then you may be found redeemable. This means you must go through the five steps above to get forgiveness. However, to your relief you mercifully will not be pulled to "Hell or Hades" to pay for your sins against mankind and now have a chance to be forgiven.

Not all souls must go through this stage. It depends upon their wrong doing in life. Most often than not, ones soul will instantly be shown the light after their passing and allowed to go into it. If you have doubt of whether or not you are worthy of moving into the light as you read this, then you need to make amends for anything bad you have done. It's apparent, you feel guilt already for something.

I always emphasize the importance of, saying your sorries before you die as opposed to trying to make amends after physical death. Get as much guilt off your shoulders now while you have time to.

Swallow your pride, redeem your sins now so it does not per say, "Haunt" you later.

Chapter 5
" Physical Death what to Expect"

We go through the dying process within many different scenarios, each having its own indifference and conclusion. Each though, reaching the same inevitable ending, a peaceful pain free passing.

Depending on the circumstances, each individual will feel different prior to their physical passing. Painful diseases will of course cause an enormous amount of pain prior to passing. Any physical illness such as stroke, heart attack or alike, will cause considerable discomfort. Also, as you are still alive, your nerve endings will still be receiving messages of pain, thus sending it to your brain. Though this sounds all so frightening and makes the prospect of dying a bit harder to handle, there is indeed not all discomfort in the dying process.

This is because dying itself, is not painful in the least. When one actually reaches those last minutes of life, the physical pain will subside and the nerves will become less responsive to the trigger of pain. Actually, the body will feel tinglier in sensation in addition, numb. There is a euphoric feeling that will overwhelm you one of peace. In some cases, you will actually be aware of your soul starting to leave your body.

Some, who have died, just experienced a feeling of standing up and walking outside their body. Others like myself, felt a numbness start at my feet and gradually go up my legs, numbing each part it had just left. Then working its way up my chest out through the top of my head. This was my soul leaving.

You see I had died once and this is what I experienced as it was happening. My soul left my body from the feet moving towards my head. It was not in the least painful at anytime during this process. At first though, after I had left my body, I could not see anything but could hear everything going on in operating room. Then it happened, a light started to appear accompanied by a feeling of moving away from my body and the room I was in. The sounds of the operating room drifted and faded away. It appeared very peaceful and in a way serene, yet I must admit a bit confusing. I was not sure at the point where I was going and felt I had little control.

If you ever watched the sunlight coming in through a window in the wee dawn hours of the morning, you would notice it attracts dust in the room, to its beams. This dust drifts aimlessly towards the source, the sunlight with little control. Well that's what I had felt. Being pulled toward that one direction the light and unable to resist it. No bigger than a piece of dust. You have total consciousness during this, being just as alert and aware as you did when inside your own body. I felt if I had continued in this manner, I would have moved through this tunnel of light, into something much more comforting and materialistic. It was not my time to go though so my journey ended abruptly and I was being pulled or drawn back into my body. It was like in reverse.

The sounds of the operating room came back loud and clear. The feeling of entering my body startled me. I once again could feel physical pain of which I knew only came with life. It was like being reborn or given a second chance. You realize thou when this re entry of soul into body happens that in order to be alive you will have to take the pain again. Others who have passed saw the light also or a tunnel like vision. All who have experienced it have said, you are drawn to it and feel you must move on. It's all so simple and easy. Unless you are weighed down.

Weighing down as I explain within this book, is the carrying of problems, guilt, fear of rendering you incapable of moving freely into the light before you at the instant of death. If this happens and you do not let go immediately of these worldly things or emotions, the light will disappear for you. This will leave you in a state of being earthbound, which can last for years until you finally get rid of or get over those earthly things that are holding you down.

When you get serious and ask "God" to help you or show you the light again, you will be able to descend into it like you are suppose to. It may take persistent pleas for help from "God" and asking for forgiveness before you will once again "See the light". Don't however, give up. Sometimes it takes time the second time around for the light.

In the meantime, if you are rendered earthbound, it could get lonely and confusing. Many earthbound souls reach up with others also lost and travel together to ease the loneliness. You have to be careful thou of those you get close to after death as some souls may not want to move into the light and can hold you down.

Some can appear domineering or controlling. Therefore, if this is the situation and you need a good friend when being earthbound, its best to stay with a more passive soul whose same wish is to also find and move on into the light. Souls on the other-side are just as they were in life. If they were good in life, so be it in death. The people who died that had nasty, controlling and almost cruel dispositions in life will be the same in death. Be selective and careful. Before you move into the light your emotions will remain very earth like. You will get mad, be happy, sing and feel fear as you did before. In other words you will still be earthly unstable!

Once you find the light a better perspective and understanding of everything, and more control over your emotions will happen. The light is redeeming and calming plus packed with pure logic and reasoning. Thus alleviating the burden of emotions, you felt in life. Love will remain intact. The only change will be the handling of such love in a more patient and logical manner. True love is eternal after physical death.

We established that emotions, consciousness remain the same after we part. If earthbound some physical sensations may remain. An abeyance of sensations may be felt. Cold, temperature change and slight sensory sensations like tingling, burning still can be felt. It's not at all painful so need to worry about that.

To sum it all up, it's quite easy and calming when you first leave your body, the light should or will be there and you should not reject it and move on. If you do not move into you shall just be basically stuck earthbound until you can let go and seek it out again. It's not death you should fear, but the pain you feel while still alive that will be the most challenging part. Soul departure from the body is the easy part.

I hope after reading this, you will feel better knowing dying is not painful.

Chapter 6
"Family left behind in heaven"

We all know that when we leave our earthly bodies and move on we leave behind the people who seem most important to us, our earthly family and friends who grieve our loss to such great extreme at times. You must also be aware that while leaving your earthly body and moving on into another level of heaven ,we are greeted and met by what appears to be strangers, yet we find we know them and love them like family. They are your family. They are your past life lovers, spouse, brothers,sisters,children and friends.

We miss our heavenly families when we are born as much as our earthly families miss us when we pass. You see we have family, friends in heaven waiting for us, missing us as we do them, without even knowing they exist, while alive on the earth.

When I was a child, small as can be I would tear up and gaze off, as if I yearned or loved someone so extremely much I could not bear it at times. Yes, I cried for them, missed them, yet had the knowledge that they were nameless, faceless and unfamiliar to me as I lived on this earth.

In every ones life, they have periods of melancholy, where out of nowhere this incredible loneliness or need will erupt into uncontrollable tears. Gazing out into an ocean does that to me. We feel we are missing someone, wanting to see them again yet unsure why or whom they are. Some people are born with this incredible sorrow of missing someone they do not even know, while living on earth. Unfortunately, the emptiness can follow them their whole lives and cause them much grief and sadness.

They may be diagnosed as suffering from manic depression, with no obvious means of why they are so depressed. All physical reasons for such distress, have been ruled out. Those suffering cannot quite understand why they are always so depressive and soon realize that nothing can alleviate that over whelming feeling. Truth be it known, that in some depression cases, notice I say some, that indeed they do miss someone from another earthly past life, or miss those from a level in heaven, from which you had spent time, before your rebirth into this life that you live now. Unfortunate, for you, that love was not suppressed on your earthly birth as much as it should have been. Mainly because true love is eternal, it never dies no matter what life you live and where.

You live many existences in different levels or planes. These are the planes of existence, levels of life both on earth as in heaven.

In death, after our earthly passing, those ready to go straight into the light; will see faces of familiar deceased relatives, from their earthly realm. We will also notice some strangers waiting for us in heaven, whom we loved, perhaps during another life of ours, or within our pre existence prior to our earthly birth, up in heaven.

Once we move on more into the light, those faces become more familiar and memories start to come back. They have been waiting for us and missing us as much as we did them. They are our families left behind in heaven before our rebirth into life.

You see, we were dead in the earthly plane, before we are born on earth and we are dead in the heavenly plane, once we are born earthly.

Summing it up,

We have both earthly and heavenly families in heaven waiting for us.

Chapter 7
"Past Lives, Reincarnation"

Reincarnation is an event of living one, or many, lives prior to your current life. We would consider these as our "Past Lives". Though many may shun off this possibility, it is indeed factual. However, new souls to this earth have not yet, participated in this cycle of life.

Our mission on earth, is to learn valuable life lessons for each existence we live. For with each lesson we learn, we can therefore escalate up the levels of heaven to a higher learning standard called " Perfection" .Though most of us go to heaven, there is in fact, many levels to it. Ten to be exact that I'm aware of. The tenth level is exact perfection, only where the most "Supreme "exist. Each level has to do with a life lesson learned. For example, one may have to learn not to be greedy and therefore exist on earth with greed in the equation.

Keeping this in mind, it will help explain, why some are rich while other souls are poor. It is all impartial and not personal in anyway, nor is it punishment from "heaven", because your in poverty, as some may think. There is a valuable lesson to be learned in being rich as there is one in being poor.

We get each chance to witness both poverty and wealth in any one of our past lives. The fact we reincarnate several times and learn life lessons from each cycle of it, explains to us, why several levels of heaven exist. Each level, as I said, reflects a valuable lesson learned.

"Why does this have anything to do with the preparing for the afterlife?" you might ask. It will aide in your transition into heaven if you are aware of what to expect and therefore making you fearless of going into the "Light". You will be less confused and not be hesitant to move on.

Each level of heaven can interact with any other level. So seeing friends and family on the other side, is a must. "Heaven" is exactly that, "Heaven" on no matter what level you will reside. However, the sins you may have committed in your previous cycle on earth may reflect onto your next earthly lives lesson. So try to be good and keep your perspective of self-righteousness in this life! Keeping in mind ," What you do in life will eventually come back at you", because it renders all so true in the afterlife…

If I have not yet convinced you of reincarnation then consider the below questions I have included. If you can answer any of them, you may have witnessed a past, life experience verifying the fact you may have lived before.

Questions to evaluate the possibility of your reincarnation:

1. Have you ever felt at any given moment, in your life an unexplainable sadness?

2. An overwhelming need for something whether it would be a person, place or time, but yet unknown?

3. Have you ever looked at a building and felt you have seen it before, even though you knew you have never been there?

4. Do you find you have extreme knowledge about an event in history, but very unaware of how you would know about it?

5. Have you ever been driven to buy an antique or artifact, from a certain era in history and not sure why?

6. Have you ever drawn a detailed picture of a person, place or thing and can not recall where you saw them?

7. Do you sometimes have flashes of memory of someone, yet not know who they are?

8. Do you feel especially drawn to a certain name but unsure why?

9. Do you have vivid dreams of a place, repeatedly, that you have never visited?

10. Have you ever felt instantly comfortable with a stranger you have just met?

11. Have you ever seen a stranger in public that grabs your attention and looks familiar to you, yet you do

not know them?

Now that you may have established whether you have been involved in a past life, here are some questions to see if you may be a new soul. You must be of adult age to answer these as these reflect the degree of maturity in ones soul.

1. Do you find ways to make things better in your life?

2. Do you use caution when making most decisions?

3. Do you take life seriously?

4. Does it bother you to see others in pain?

5. Do you sometimes think of ways you could help others?

6. If going on a long/short trip, do you carefully plan the details?

7. Do you check, when retiring for the night, appliances are off, doors are locked?

8. When someone tells you to do something, do you first think of reasons why not too?

9. Do you NOT believe everything you read or hear?

10. Do you try to put others first before yourself?

If you answered yes to most, if not all these questions, chances are you have an educated older soul. If you answered yes to only a two, you may be a newer soul.

Most with new souls are somewhat unaware of any destructive obstacles in life. They are less prepared for different scenarios or situations in life. They are somewhat naive in situations and confrontations with others. They greatly lack the knowledge to plan things out. Human tragedy may not affect them as diversely as an older soul. They feel little empathy with others pain though not completely without some sympathetic feelings.

A newer soul acts more on impulse than on thought. Common sense may not prevail although they may be highly intelligent intellectually. A new soul has learned little, if none of, lessons in life pertaining to greed, lust, love, honesty, compassion or trust. Its not that they are bad, just uneducated and in the early learning process of life. Nothing seems too serious to them, unless it affects them, personally and diversely.

On the other hand, an older well-educated soul will be more aware of their surroundings, prepared for most situations and utilizes common sense decisions daily. They have learned most lessons in life and know how to proceed cautiously, yet not too extremely.

Hopefully by now, from reading this chapter, you will know if you are indeed an older wiser soul.

If you have acknowledge that fact, you will understand that this is just one of your many lives you have lived and that reincarnation is indeed, a fact of life.

As I always say and truly believe, "There is no end to us".

Chapter 8
"What's on the planes in Heaven"

After much research and communication with the deceased on the other-side via audio recording sessions, I have come to a certain conclusion that heaven is definitely made up of several levels. I estimated there are 10 levels of heaven, perhaps more. The first level being the youngest and the tenth being for only the most Supreme, where God and thy Saints reside. Though one may go to heaven after their passing on earth, they will probably not, reside on the same level as "God" himself. This is only for the "Supreme". The lower levels are according to how well you performed on earth, age of soul, and what lessons you have already learned.

Each level has its own class or course of education according to how well educated people are in the lessons learned and skills needed to become the best one can be under "God".Each level or plane in heaven is almost a carbon copy of earth. There are seas, lakes, blue skies, and grass, just as on earth. There are stores, houses, schools whatever you need is there. It is as I have been told cheerfully bright and incredibly peaceful and carefree. There is virtually no crime or threat of it as those who reside there gain a certain respect for humanity. What I mean by that is, that all are related and friends amongst one another on each plane of heaven, so there is no indifference. Only unity can be seen and felt.

You are given more free choice of what home you would like to reside in while in heaven. This is because in heaven we are more aware that material things are not so important thus letting us choose our home according to our hearts desire, not the prestige of owning it. If you want a garden, you shall have one as long as it is something you want and not selected solely for the purpose to impress others.

Yes, dreams can come true in heaven. What may have been important to you in life will not be so in heaven, so your choices will be simpler and overall more satisfying. Family may reside in heaven but not necessarily on the same plane. Depends on the needs and age of the individual soul. This does not mean if you reside on the 8th plane, you can not visit with grandpa on the 9th! Another point to bring up is you will have many heavenly families from different existences you had lived both previously on earth and in heaven. Previous families, you will not remember until you move on after your past earthly life and enter back into heaven. You will never be alone.

I was informed that I am from Level 9 plane in heaven. Also from the deceased, I learned that others miss me and reside in that plane (level) of heaven, waiting my return. Its reassuring to know I will not be alone once I do return to my heavenly home. It is also reassuring to hear voices from those that have past that there is life beyond mortal physical death and there is no end to us.

I would like to mention why we are put on different planes in heaven and how that is decided. According to the information I have gathered and observations on my part, we all live several lives in our existence as a soul. This means each rebirth on earth is for educational purposes of which to better ourselves and gain the knowledge needed for perfection. So one may be rich in their earthly life but only for the reason of learning humility or greed. A lesson that need be learned by that soul. It does not necessarily mean a wealthy person in life is being rewarded for some reason or another. It just means there's a lesson learned for every earthly action. So do not feel left out in life if you are poor and someone else is wealthy.

At one point in your existence you were or will be too if you have not learned that lesson yet. Every action in life has a purpose. Now taking that into account, we live many earthly lives. Each life teaches us a new lesson. If a soul does not learn from that lesson that was put before them to be learned, then they must redo it and will not escalate up the heavenly plane until they do.

When a child dies they may not necessarily be a new soul. They may be actually a very old one .Keeping this in mind a child who has passed may not go to the 1st plane as one might think. The first level of heaven is for the new souls that are uneducated and need to learn more. They have not lived long as a soul and have little too no life experiences.

I am hoping this all makes sense to you now. If it does, you may not necessarily feel sadden life has been hard on you more so than others. Hopefully you will realize you need to learn a specific lesson from life in order to move on.

Keeping that in mind, ask yourself what you have learned from life situations and trials you have had to face. Its all for the in betterment of your soul. Continuing education in heaven also helps us escalate up the ladder of perfection. As I said before, each level or plane of heaven has schools to teach you more about what you have learned. Each school is appropriated to each plane of heaven to teach a certain level of consciousness and awareness for that specific level. Thus meaning if you have learned humility and graduated to the 9th level then you will have a review of that lesson to make sure have correctly learned and understood its full meaning.

From reading and reviewing this chapter, you should have a greater knowledge now of what to expect after death and also have come to the conclusion that "There is no end to us".

Chapter 9
"Shadows, Ghosts, Spirit, Apparitions what they are."

Once we die, we are made up mostly of energy and electricity. There are several kinds of ghosts that can appear or be seen occasionally to a living person.

Energy spirit; which will appear as a ball or a streak occasionally in color but mostly white. These energy spirits are active in flight and do not appear in a human form. They use what energy is in the air and usually cannot manifest entirely into a whole form. Not always visual to the human eye, they can be captured more easily on cameras and appear in photos as orbs, funnels or streaks. I see them as a human spirit in flight.

They are spirits not too long into death and still have the strength and spark in their souls. That is why they appear brighter. I feel these spirits in flight can move/manipulate objects causing poltergeist like activity, more easily than other spirits.

Shadow ghost; Shadow ghosts appear to people as dark, mostly in a black shadow form, with no real defining features. These spirits are very old and that is why they are so dark. Spirits of this nature may have also had a traumatic death. There is nothing sinister about them. They usually are seen out of the corner of the human eye, but on occasion's straight in front. These souls have been earthbound for an extremely long time and basically have lost their spark. Usually very passive and weak.

Residue apparition; Residue apparition is like energy left in a space in time. They do not have intelligence and will not interact with you or even acknowledge you. Always, a residue haunting is like a movie playing repeatedly.

They follow the same paths usually and cannot interact with the living. They are just a memory, planted in the atmosphere. Though completely harmless, none the less, they can still be very frightening to those who witness them.

Full bodied Apparition; a full-bodied apparition can appear in a white glow, or as in human fleshy form fully dressed in attire. The living easily sees them; however, they cannot stay manifested too long. It uses a great deal of energy for them to appear which can quickly weaken and make them disappear. These apparitions can interact with the living. You may hear them talk and openly gaze at you. They are just people like anyone living, who have passed and they carry their temperament with them. To say they are harmless would be not be logical. In life, there is good and bad people, so in death the apparition will still have the same disposition as they did in life. It depends on what type of person they were in life. It is like a living stranger coming into your home and you do not know whether they have bad intentions or not.

More times than not, the apparition is completely harmless. Even if they were of a bad disposition, it would take an awful lot of energy for them to be aggressive, which they usually do not have. These spirits can be either young or old into death. They have the intelligence of how to use their energy to appear entirely and may often utilize that knowledge.

Sinister Spirit; These may be confused as demons as they seem strong, hostile and aggressive, but are in fact not. These entities, can be seen, heard and felt. Sinister Spirits are dangerous to a certain extent, but also do have their limitations. It's best if you encounter this type of spirit, not to challenge it or intentionally anger it anymore. It is already angered and basically hates everyone, no matter what age or sex. These types of spirits were bad in life and usually carry a big chip on their shoulder you might say, when entered into death. Occasionally they were humans abused or murdered who soul reason for haunting is to seek revenge. Most often though they are just nasty souls who treated people badly in life with little remorse. Unfortunately the innocent living become victims of that rage. They may grunt, growl or curse which makes them appear demon like, thou they are not. Often they play mind games with the living as a control thing, by taunting or teasing them to get a reaction. They can cause depression in the living and then feed from that negative energy. They can manipulate your moods and make meek man anger easily. If you have to deal with this type of entity, it is best to get some professional help for removal.

Removal may be accomplished mostly, if the homeowner persistently ignores the spirits attempts to torment others and performs a house cleansing on daily basis. Making a spirit, whether good or bad, feel uncomfortable on a daily basis can make them give up and move on. You have to be persistent with this though, possibly everyday for weeks or months. Certain herbs, salt, crosses even rocks, may weaken their desire to stay. Daily prayers to Saint Michael may help. Also, though it may be hard, try not to acknowledge them. Soon they may become bored if you do not interact or react to their taunts. Hopefully, they will feel uncomfortable, from your efforts so much they move on.

Atmospheric manipulation spirit; Weakened spirit little or no energy force. It cannot manifest or be seen but can cause temperature changes, or disturbances in the atmosphere. You may feel your hair stand up on your arms, a breath of air move past you or at you, or get cold chills. A general feeling of not being alone can overpower you. Not usually a new spirit, but mostly a failing old entity. This is due to extreme energy loss because of it being earthbound for a long time. Eventually, these spirits fade entirely away never to be felt again. Non aggressive and weak.

Half Spirit; Cannot fully form into full body apparition. Weaker energy force than a full apparition ghost. They may have the knowledge of how to manifest but not the energy source to do so completely. May appear as smokey, swirls or mist. Intelligent, can partially interact with the living and aware of its surroundings. No time frame of being earthbound of this specter, though my estimate is newly deceased - mid deceased. Usually harmless. Sometimes a family member.

Caged Ghost; Spirit trapped by memory, environment or will of their own. Only seen in one location. Fearful to move past that location. Usually spirit is over whelmed by fear, sadness, or a structural restriction. Past traumatic situation such as a war or sudden lost of life can hold them there. Also, the environment such as a steel or metal ship can cause soul to be unable to leave. Commitment also to a person, place or object can cause restraint. Their energy is usually fueled by their fear and/or emotions. Can be seen on occasions. Harmless.

Chapter 10
"Real Death Scenario"

Occasionally, through my visitations from those that have passed on and recordings of their voices, I come across detailed conversations of their experiences on the other side.

One sad case I was practically impressed with. The details of the entire journey just before and after death unfolded to me with precise details, step by step, of what they went through. I recorded their voices, for information and now have them on a cd to sell to the public. Most information I received is not however, included on the cd. Some of the information, if not most, was too private to be revealed to the public.

The real life death scenario unfolded unto the life of two young men. I will not say in which state this happened or the names of the victims. Apparently, the two young men were bored and went cruising, as they said. The one young man, the driver of the car was adventurous, hyperactive, sarcastic in nature and a bit controlling of the other male passenger. He had the leader type, bully type qualities throughout high school.

The male passenger became at the mercy of the rebellious driver. The passenger was a very mild natured young man, who knew right from wrong usually but had a tendency to be a follower. His passive nature was no match for the drivers temper and controlling nature. The male driver admitted to me he was speeding and ignored his passengers' pleas to slow down. He found it all so humorous to ignore his friend and be in control.

At one point, his speed matched over 85 MPR on a road with slight curves. It had been raining the night before and a few puddles were still visible on the road in low-lying spots. He lost control after hitting a puddle and swerved a few times trying to control the automobile but was unsuccessful. The car flipped several times finally resting on its hood. Neither young men had seatbelts on and were thrown about, I am not certain on this one point, but one may have been thrown out of the car. Then they said all went black for them. They had consciousness but no vision. They had both just entered into death.

At first, they said it was quiet and total darkness yet they had a certain amount of awareness. Then they said it got lighter and they both found themselves standing (not hovering), outside the vehicle looking at it. At first, they thought they had survived the crash as it all happened so fast. It was not until the police came that they truly understood they were dead. Several reasons led to that conclusion, one being the police would not acknowledge the two young men's presence or reply when they were trying to communicate. Then they could see visually, their own body's .Some details from that point are a bit vague for me, as they did not fill me in on everything that unfolded.

They were aware of a light at that point and felt the need to go into it, but the stronger of the two men held the meeker one back from doing so. Apparently, the driver knew it was his fault, the accident, and felt he was responsible for his friends' death, therefore a murderer. He thought he would surely go to "Hell" for his crime. His controlling nature was still present.

As I explained before, you carry your personalities with you in death and very little changes. However, things will start unfolding before you, sins you committed in life and once you pass you have to deal with that guilt. The driver instantaneously tried to control the passenger after their passing. Fearing he would be punished for causing the death of his friend, he held him back from going into the light.

According to the passenger, the driver also did not want to be left alone through this journey. Apparently, they wandered aimlessly, without any direction for a long period. Both had become lost souls. Eventually, they met up with a group of other souls trapped and just as bewildered as them on where to go. They traveled together to try to find someone who could help them.

Certain living people have an aura around them and avian of guidance and compassion. They are called sensitives and empathics, like myself. An empathic living person is like a beacon of goodwill to a deceased soul. The souls feel they can get help and guidance from a sensitive/empathic. On this particular occasion, these two young men and the group they were with had found me. I had the qualities that attracted them while they were passing through my area. I felt the presence of the group immediately and their emotions. I knew they were lost and needed help but had to devise away to communicate with them.

I am able to feel their emotions, sense their needs but I cannot actually hear them. On occasion in my life, I have heard them but very few times, usually if I did it was as a child. Therefore, because I was doing audio analyzing, which is recording the naturally white noise within a room, I decided to try to record these unexpected visitors' voices. With the use of a microphone, good audio equipment and the group of lost souls visiting me, it was easily successful. I started my sessions to the group, by asking questions and got some incredible answers. I also recorded the two young men from the accident quarreling together. The driver seem to give me sarcastic answers, were as the passenger apologized to me, for him, when he did.

The passenger talked the most of needing help, his love for his father and his friends' fear of being punished for the accident. He also told me of the accident before and after. I sensed his fear of his friend. It became apparent the passenger wanted to see the light again and move on. One EVP I recorded begged me to please show and bring him the light again.

My job as a spiritual investigator is too help those lost souls cross over into the light. To do that in this particular case, I had to convince the driver he was safe from punishment. If he had not been grabbed after first few minutes of death and dragged below, he would be safe. That is how it happens, if you have sinned badly, almost immediately after death. I started to get recordings of the drivers' voice calming down and feeling remorse. He believed me and decided to let go of his friend.

I said a prayer, for the light to be shown, asked for forgiveness for their sins and felt them, finally gently leave. It was finally over. The rest of the group they had traveled with left also into the light. My home became quiet and empty again. Now to some this story might seem unbelievable thou it is all so true. This is a true story of two young men who passed and their journey.

Being a sensitive/empathic like all things needs some training to perfect. Unfortunately, there are no teachers pertaining to this special talent. The individual, like me, has to see, feel and figure out how to do this job on his or her own. I had to practice and teach myself, how to correctly, efficiently, send spirits into the light. It took years of trial and error to perfect this special gift into an efficient professional career. I had to be sure I did everything correctly, as I am helping the lost souls of real people. Their demise depended completely on me.

I am truly grateful and feel it very rewarding that I can help these lost souls, after all someone has to!

Chapter 11
"Why do some Souls Haunt?"

Souls that have passed from this life and have not moved directly into the light become earthbound. Once souls become earthbound , they have no ideal where to go. Their homestead may become a past dwelling they lived in when still alive. If they find a living person who has an aura about them of compassion they may choose to reside in that persons home. This would be mainly for the purpose of getting help. Other motives for a haunting in a home may be because of an object. Something they may have cherished in life you have bought and brought into your home.

A strong attachment to an object is one of the many reasons a soul may be unable to move on. It could be the location of which they naturally died in or a place they were murdered and felt great pain in.. It may also be a place that is abandoned as they do not want to disturb anybody or be disturbed. Also a lost soul may choose the place that once was where their last love lived. A past job location could also become their home. Sometimes a earthy dedication to a job or profession can weigh a spirit down. Last but not least, is the cemetery where they were buried. It's the last place and only place their body has remained since they left it.

In any case, the location a soul may inhabit after death holds some kind of memories related to their life lost. Once they take up space in a dwelling, for whatever reason, they still need help to move on. They find they have gotten bored with the situation and restless. Since communication with the living is nearly impossible for them, they diligently try to find other ways to communicate with the living. This is where the term "haunting" comes into play.

Eventually, these souls may find an alternative way to communicate with the living other than speech. The soul still embraces the will it had in life to do things. The way they use this will is by utilizing their energy force within or draining from an outside energy source. This can be managed through various objects in a home mostly ones that contribute electricity such as an appliance, or a source that conducts electricity such as a generator or battery. The soul both in the living and dead , is made up of a certain level of electricity itself as in static electricity. Since the spirit has some use of its own electricity it may need more and therefore that is why it drains from an outside its own souls capability. Also, stealing a living persons energy may become an objective for them. The living victim of this mischievous energy stealing thief will feel drained and tired once their energy has been stolen.

Once the spirit learns how to utilize their own energy combining it with an outside source, they will find and yet be limited to manipulation & movement of an object. These are the sounds you may hear in the quiet of the night or even during bright daylight hours within your home if it is haunted. The souls of people whom have passed get lonely if unable to co-exist and communicate with others. They are only human. They want people to know they are around. Sometimes though, a deceased soul may not want to be found and hide. In that case they may have a fear that overwhelms them of the living, death itself or a past memory. These souls could dwell in a home and go completely unnoticed.

The ones though that make themselves known through noises, footsteps, bangs and yes sometimes a visual appearance are demanding your attention. They want you to notice them. That is how they are communicating to the homeowner. Its like saying "Hi, I am here notice me" but through actions not words.

To explain it more clearly a soul of a human being once they have died, no longer has a voice box to communicate and has to find a more efficient way to communicate to suit their specific needs. The spirit may appear to be menacing to the homeowner but it is basically not meant to appear so aggressive or menacing . In the case of a sinister spirit who seems aggressive the best thing to do is not acknowledge them. Do not let them feed off your fear.

However in the case of just a lonely spirit who wants some attention., speaking to them may help or bring them comfort. Explain to them that this is your home and you would like to set some rules if they are to remain. Also, expressing sympathy towards the lost soul could help enormously! Tell them you are sorry they died and you care for their well-being. Convince them that they got family in the light waiting for them. Also, remind them if they have sinned that they will be forgiven if they move into the light and they have nothing to fear. As I said before, if they were to be punished it would have happened immediately after they departed.

One could also at this point call for "God" to show the soul the light, to forgive their sins and allow them to move into it. This is how I help spirits to move on. So far it has worked in every case I've had to move them on. Main thing is to reassure them they will not be punished. They are scared to move on for some reason, I speculate mostly because of guilt. When one really thinks about it, such as myself, I really feel sorry for these spirits that are earthbound. They're just people who do not know where to go once they have passed., because they have missed the initial light that was shown to them. These souls retain their personalities and cry or get upset just like any other human being .

We as human beings ourselves, need to realize they are in need of our help. We need to open up that door between life and death, get rid of our inhabitations, fears and safety zones of perception and let our sympathy , empathy prevail for these are fellow human beings . Then we need to try to help them move on. They so need our help. Someone once said to me, "What is really scary is the fact it could be a member of our own family trapped and earthbound". How horrific that thought is!

I do know one thing, if that was my family member stuck in limbo, I would be ever so grateful if whom-ever alive comes in contact with them, could or would ,help them move on! In a way when looking at these lost souls as potentially one of your own family members trapped earthbound, it makes you realize you do have empathy, sympathy for them. That they are only people. So the next time you encounter one of these specters, perhaps you will be more educated and approach the occurrence with more compassion and knowledge of just what they are going through and their need to move on.

Most importantly they need YOUR help.

Chapter 12
"Help me be a better person"

"How does one eliminate the chances of becoming earthbound or lost after death?" you may ask. The key to keeping heavy earthly weights from bogging you down after death is to control your life and social behaviors with grace, patience, compassion, love and humility.

1. Take every object you own as a gift not as an award. You are not exceptional because you have these things but only humble to have received them. Be appreciative for what you have and combine it with a little humility, be grateful but do not gleam of greatness. Do not boast of your possessions to others or use it as a way to be superior or as a devise to belittle someone else.

2. Have compassion for others as you would have for yourself or your immediate family. Lend a helping hand, support, if need be. A good ear is comforting if someone just needs to talk. If you are financially able and find another human in financial turmoil, share with them what you can as a courteously and an act of compassion, not as a loan. If you can help, do not turn your back on their needs before you.

3. Do not attempt to be a "god" or superior against another person. Do not control their destiny by firing, laying off, degrading or depriving another individual of their rights to work or exist. Personal feelings of dislike are not a sufficient reason to fire someone from their job. Taking away a job could have drastic consequences to the family of the one being fired.

Loss of medical insurance because of a lay off or unaccredited firing can cost an unhealthy family member their life. Loss of money into the household can leave innocent children starving. Families could lose their home and become homeless. Think before you decide to lay off or fire an otherwise studious and hard working employee. Their future could be in your hands and though you may never see them again, the effects of your actions could cause turmoil for them the rest of their lives. This you could and would be liable for after you die.

4. Never intentionally hurt another human being. Harsh words and name-calling are included in this. Compliment others as much as you can. If angry, turn it into a compliment but not into an adverse action of anger. Lean instead of push. Be humble. Do not ever strike another person with hatred. There's always another way out, be open and listen to what they have to say. Apologize if need be in a calming, controlled manner. No matter who thinks they're right in a verbal argument the only one who truly is, is the forgiver.

5. If you have caused pain against any other in any way or manner, apologize if possible before your physical passing. Guilt lays heavy on the soul. Say what you need to say in an appropriate manner. Feel remorse for what you have done and reconcile with the victim of your cruelty with compassionate and favorable words. If you leave this world knowing you did your best to be humane and compassionate of others your soul will be lighter and free of guilt. Your entry into heaven would be secure and the initial light will be there for you after your passing. All ones' soul would have to do further ,is let go of their earthly life and memories and receive the light with grace. Being willing and ready to go into it, should prevail.

Everyone in their life has something they did that they feel regret for. Mere awareness of your bad deed will not compensate for the pain you may have afflicted upon another. You will have plenty of awareness of all you did wrong in the afterlife, but zero opportunity to apologize and bring closure.

In rare occasions there has been instances when someone has died due to their own bad judgment. I have handle cases with clients in past that involved a haunting of a deceased love one who had died because of a bad decision made on their part. In all cases of these haunting, the loved one who passed had ignored the spouses pleas not to do it. They did it anyway and ended up dying because they did. After their death they felt a horrendous guilt for not listening to their spouse. They wanted to apologize but no longer could communicate with them. They began to try to get their spouses attention by basically haunting their home. Usually the client had gone through several different paranormal teams before they had found me.

Once I was brought into the case I could read from the impressions and feelings of the deceased spouse. I realized all they wanted to do was say they were sorry. Once I conveyed this message to the surviving spouse and they in turn vocally replied back "It is alright, you are forgiven", the spirit could then move on. There is not many instances where a person like myself, with my skills, could be called upon to intervene .

In most cases like this the spirit would become earthbound because of guilt and not move on. It is important we listen to our loved ones requests to protect us from any harm, when they offer it. I always say that if you do not feel completely sure about the safety when doing something, do NOT do it. Being a better person also means using common sense decisions as part of your everyday life.

In conclusion:

By following my guidelines above on how to become a better person ,there should little trouble receiving and entering the light after one passes. Its all up to you. You and only you control your destiny.

Chapter 13
"Conclusion what we have Learned "

Let us review the whole cycle of death and what this book should have taught you. To do this we start with basics and at the beginning sequence of death. Death sounds like such a harsh word, almost incriminating.

As we should have learned from this book, it is not in fact so disturbing, nor does physical death mean the ending of ones life. This information should have proven that we do indeed live on, forever. Our time on earth is just a small phase of our continual cycle of life, almost as vast as a gentle breeze in the air flowing into a destination unknown... It never ends. The soul passing from the body is indeed not painful nor ending. We simply leave the house we live in because it has broken down and it no longer is livable. After we move out, we no longer feel physical pain.

We are greeted by a light or a strong will to move on. What we see may be darkness at first no more menacing than if one was to shut their eyes and fall asleep. In that brief period of darkness a light should gradually appear. It is at this time one should please ask "God" to bring them into the light. Another thing you should have learned from this book is to immediately let go of your earthly life.

Any thoughts of family, your life or things you have done in your life should be pushed aside. This early moment of death is not the time to reminisce. You can do that later. Your main goal should be to find resolution, reassurance and direction in your new home heaven. If by chance, you do not move into the light it can fade away. You will become weighted down and therefore need to find out what it is that laying heavy on your soul.

This would be whether it's guilt, or an attachment to a person, place job, or item. There are three scenarios after you pass.

1. You go into the light and give up all other earthly things freely (for the time being).

2. You reject the light and become earthbound by choice

3. You have been found unredeemable because of an evil deed and sent below immediately.

The first two options depend on what your state of conscious is after you pass. Whether you are dependent on you earthly life and body or not. Once you reject the light, you must try to find it again. Otherwise, you will not know where to go. Please do not make haunting a home an option! We all deserve so much better than that. It's not living its being in limbo. Not alive and not yet collectively earthly dead. You need to move into the light if you are earthbound.

To refresh what I have said, one needs to find out what is holding them here and let go. Then, that earthbound soul must call to "God" to ask for forgiveness for any sins and to please show you the light again. Also again, this may take several attempts for "God" to find you. You can use (call) the names of all supreme in heaven if you have not yet been acknowledged and no light is visible. This includes saints. Once you finally see that light again immediately, go into it. Do not look back. The light may seem tunnel like or like a ray of soothing warm light. One going into the light will feel light and may seem to drift without will, into it.

At the end of the light as it gets brighter and with permanence, you will/ may be greeted by family, whether from the most recent life you lived or a previous life before. You may even get a glimmer of the supreme himself, "God". Once you are totally inside the light, you will feel overwhelming happiness. All earthly weights will be lifted. You will still remember your life, but will be able to handle those memories in a more sensible way. You will reconnect with friends and families and be given time to adjust before moving on fully.

As I said, there are levels in heaven one of which you will take residence on. It will be absolutely stunning and bright, beautiful and calming in ways one could never imagine. You may have to meet with someone and tell him or her what you have learned. This will help decide your placement level in heaven.

Once the entry into heaven has been acknowledge and received, decisions will be reviewed and you will move in appropriately to the level you should be on. It cannot be bad again once you have entered. No more pain, inhibitions, guilt, anger, resentment or bad will of any nature will be present in you. You will be heavenly free! The plane or level of heaven you will be assigned to will have everything you need.

Your only requirement will be to review what you have learned and perhaps attend a school to perfect that particular life lesson. From then on, it will be wonderful! Earthly time passes faster in heaven. You will see relatives grow and depart their earthly bodies in a faster time than by earth years. Eventually you will all be together again in heaven… Yes, you can check on your family members still alive on earth! It's all in the equation. Your love for them is eternal.

In conclusion, it will all go simply and efficiently if you let it when you first pass from your body.

Because there is "No end to us" ever, you must move on.

Book References

For more information about the author, website, book and "Spirit Voices" Cd, please visit our website at; http://www.spookmanor.com

Special thanks to; spookmanor.com Productions & Paranormal Investigations and its dedicated friends & associates 2010